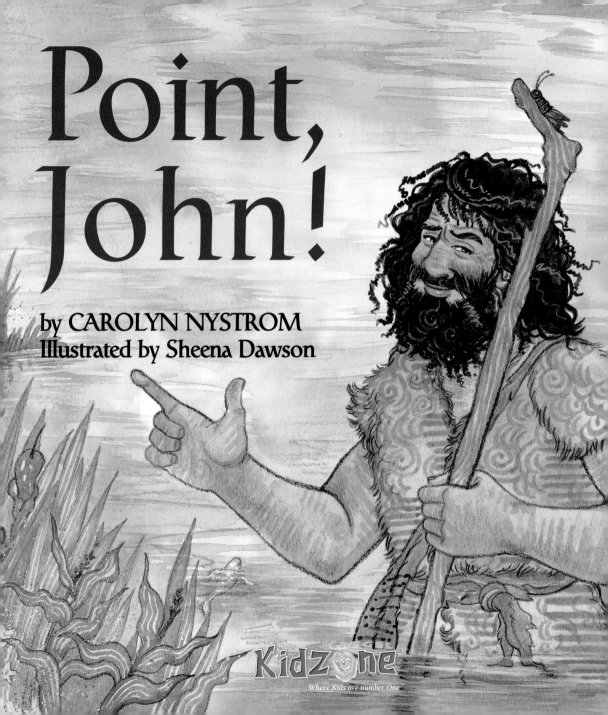

# Point, John!

by CAROLYN NYSTROM
Illustrated by Sheena Dawson

KIDZONE
Where Kids are number One

Text © 2004 Carolyn Nystrom
Illustrations © 2004 Angus Hudson Ltd/Tim Dowley &
Peter Wyart trading as Three's Company

Published in the USA by Kregel Publications 2004
Distributed by Kregel Publications,
Grand Rapids, Michigan 49501

Learn more about John in Matthew 3:1–17; 11:1–9; Mark
1:1–11; 6:14–29; Luke 1:1–80; 3:1–20; 7:18–35; and
John 1:19–34.

ISBN 0-8254-3334-7

Worldwide co-edition produced by Lion Hudson plc,
Mayfield House, 256 Banbury Road,
Oxford OX2 7DH,
Tel: +44 (0) 1865 302750
Fax: +44 (0) 1865 302757
e-mail: coed@lionhudson.com
www.lionhudson.com

Printed in China

04 05 06 07 08 / 5 4 3 2 1

I know that I'm a strange-looking man.
I wear camel's hair clothes
and dried camel's hide for a belt.
I eat locusts and other bugs for food—
with a drizzle of wild honey.
I live outdoors in a hot desert.
I do all this because God gave me a special job.
My name is John. They call me "the Baptist."

3

"Repent!" I yelled to the crowds.
"You have done everything wrong!
You have sinned. Tell God you are sorry.
He will forgive you.
The kingdom of heaven is near.
You must get ready! Now!"

I watched the people.
Some covered their ears
and ran away.
(Yes, I know I was loud.)
But others came to me.
I baptized them in the Jordan River
to show that God was washing
away their sins.

I was loud. I was fast.
But I knew I did not have long to preach.
I was born to point to someone else.

Here is the story my parents told me
when I was three, and five, and seven, and eleven.

My father served in the temple.
One day, while he was burning incense on God's altar,
he felt something (or someone) nearby.
He looked up and shook with fear.
An angel stood right next to the altar!

"Don't be afraid," the angel said.
"God has heard your prayers."
"W-w-which prayers?" my father stammered.
"God will give you a son," the angel said.
"But Elizabeth and I are too old," my father said.
The angel just smiled. "Name him John," he said.

"Your son will bring people back to God.
He will be as strong as the great prophet Elijah."
"How can I be sure of this?" my father asked.
"You will not be able to say one word
until your son is born," the angel said.
"My name is Gabriel."
Then the angel disappeared.

7

Six months later my mother's belly was large.
One day she heard a soft knock at the door.
"Mary!" she gasped in surprise.
Then she held her belly and laughed.
"I guess my baby is saying 'hi' too."

All day the two women whispered their secrets.
Mary had also seen an angel.
She was going to have a baby too.
But there was one big difference.
Mary's baby was the Son of God.

"My soul glorifies the Lord," sang Mary.
"My spirit rejoices in God my Savior."
Slowly, my mother began to understand my job.

Mary stayed with us until I was born.
When I was eight days old, all our friends came for a party.
It was time to give me a name.
"He looks like his dad," said one.
"Maybe we should call him Zechariah."
Everyone laughed and clapped.
"Zechariah is a good name," they all said.
"No!" shouted my mother.
Everything got still.
"We should call him John," she said quietly.

"What will his father think?" said one man.
My dad waved for something to write on,
because he still couldn't talk.
*H-i-s n-a-m-e i-s J-o-h-n,*
wrote my dad.

And suddenly my dad was talking again,
talking about how wonderful God is—
and the important job that God would give
me to do.

"Praise the Lord, the God of Israel," he sang.
"He is coming to save his people."
(My mother glanced at Mary's belly.)
"What God promised long ago,
now he will do it!" my dad ended with a roar.

"And you, my child,"
he gently cupped my face in his hands,
"you will point to him.
You will tell his people to get ready.
And everyone will see the
power of God."

I grew to be a strong man.
God's Spirit got me ready to do his work.

"You snakes!" I shouted one day.
(I had just spotted some religious leaders in the crowd.)
"What makes you think God won't punish you?
Stop doing wrong.
You think that just because you are religious Jews,
God will take care of you.
Bah!" I spat. "See these rocks?
God could turn these rocks into people like you!"
I saw them fall back in shock.
Nobody talked to them like that.
But I knew they needed to think of someone
more important than themselves.

"Get ready," I shouted. "I baptize with water,
but someone is coming who will
baptize with fire!
I'm not good enough to untie his sandals—
and neither are you."

I did not make many friends that day.

"What shall we do to get ready?" asked a young man.
"Do you have two coats?" I asked.
He nodded.
"Give one to someone who is cold."

"Teacher, what should I do?" asked a man who collected taxes.
"Take only the tax money," I said.
"Don't keep any money for yourself."
*Yes, I know you will be poor,* I thought.

A young soldier said, "How can I get ready?"
"Don't tell lies to get people in trouble," I said.
"And," I smiled, "be happy with your pay."

"Who are you?" someone whispered.
"Are you the Christ?"
"No, I am not," I said.
"I am a voice shouting in the desert,
'Get the road ready for the Lord.'"

The next day I saw a familiar figure coming toward me.
*It's Jesus!* I said to myself, *Mary's son.*
*This is why I was born.* I pointed toward Jesus.
"Look!" I shouted to the people. "This is the
Lamb of God. He takes away the sin of the world!"
Every head turned toward Jesus.
Jesus kept walking toward me until he stood
with me in the water.
"No," I whispered, my voice hoarse.
"I shouldn't baptize you; *you* should baptize me."
"I want you to baptize me," Jesus said.
        "It is my Father's will."
        With all the people standing around,
        some of them still wet from their own baptism,
        I baptized Jesus Christ.

As soon as he came out of the water,
Jesus began to pray.
Then I saw an opening in the sky.
I saw a beautiful dove come down
and hover right over Jesus' head.
I knew this dove was a sign of God's Spirit.
Then I heard a thundering voice from heaven:
"This is my Son. He pleases me.
I love him."
Then Jesus walked away into the desert.
Some of my friends went with him.
I knew that my job was nearly done.

One day while I was teaching and baptizing,
I heard a strange noise.
"Make way! Make way!" came shouts.
"The king is coming! The king is coming!"
Soon I saw a gold carriage.
Out tumbled King Herod.
(He was fat and needed a lot of help.)
Herod straightened his clothes and his crown.
Then he walked toward me.

23

"So, what have you got to say today?" he sneered.
"I've come to see your show.
Is anybody getting wet?"

"I am baptizing only those who want to stop sinning," I said.
"Do you want me to baptize you?
Do you want to turn away from sin?"
"Me? Sin?" he laughed.
"You stole your brother's wife," I whispered in his ear.
He pushed me away.
"The king stole his brother's wife,"
I shouted to the crowd.

Those words landed me in jail.

My friends came to visit me in prison.
Sometimes they brought me food.
Sometimes we prayed.
But many of my friends stayed with Jesus.
I knew my time to live was short.

Once I had a surprising guest.
King Herod came and sat beside me.
"Have I really done wrong?" he asked.
"Can God really forgive me?"
"Jesus has come," I said.
"He is God's Son.
He can take away your sins."

But I'm not sure the king believed me.

I was in jail a long time.
I kept hearing about Jesus.
I knew that he was teaching,
that people followed him.
*But is Jesus the One?* I wondered.
*Is he really God's Son?*
I sent my friends to ask him.

Jesus told my friends,
"Stay for a while. Watch. Listen.
Then go and tell John what you see and hear.
The blind can see again. The lame walk.
The sick get well. The deaf hear.
The poor receive God's good news."

Then Jesus sent a personal message to me.
He said, "Keep on believing.
You have done your job.
You have pointed to me.
You have finished well."

I smiled and nodded to myself.
*He must increase, but I must decrease,*
I thought.
*I have done the job I was born to do.*

I remembered the words of our great prophet Isaiah,
*A voice is calling, "Clear the way for the LORD in the*
*wilderness, make smooth in the desert a highway for our*
*God."* (Isa. 40:3)

I knew that Isaiah was talking about me.